Whatever

RAIN

Lauren Taylor

Editor: Alexandra Koken
Designer: Melissa Alaverdy
Educational consultants:
    Jillian Harker and
    Heather Adamson

Copyright © QED Publishing 2013

First published in the UK in 2013
by QED Publishing
A Quarto Group Company
230 City Road,
London EC1V 2TT

www.qed-publishing.co.uk

ISBN 978 1 78171 220 7

A catalogue record
for this book is
available from
the British Library

Printed in China

Picture credits
(t=top, b=bottom, l=left, r=right,
c=centre, fc=front cover)

Alamy; 4 Wild Pictures; 12 Danita
Delimont; 14-15 Images of Africa
Photo Bank,
Dreamstime; 10r Alexeys; 11
Plampy;
Getty Images; 20-21 Michael
Cizek
Shutterstock; front cover Vaclav
Volrab; 1-2 J Paget R F Photos; 5t
Andrcivc88, 5b Dmitry Naumer;
6-7; 6b Max Topchii, 7c Greenland;
8-9 Maksim Shmeljor, 9c Soleilc;
10l Karram, 10b Acik; 16-17
Kzenon; 18-19 18t Allison 18b,
Stephane Bidouze, 19 Ralph
Loesche; 22t Neda; 22c Algecirino;
24 Jackiso

Words in **bold**
can be found in
the Glossary on
page 24.

Contents

Rain

There are many kinds of rain.

Light rain is called **drizzle**.

Thunderstorms make heavy rain. It can rain all day or just for a few minutes.

Why do we need rain?

Rain is important. Without rain, there would be no rivers or lakes. Animals, fish and birds need water.

People use water
to drink, wash
and cook.

Why does it rain?

Rain comes from **clouds** in the sky. A cloud is a group of water droplets.

When the raindrops are heavy, they fall to the ground. This is rain.

Thunderstorms

Thunderstorms have **thunder**, **lightning** and heavy rain.

thunder

lightning

heavy rain

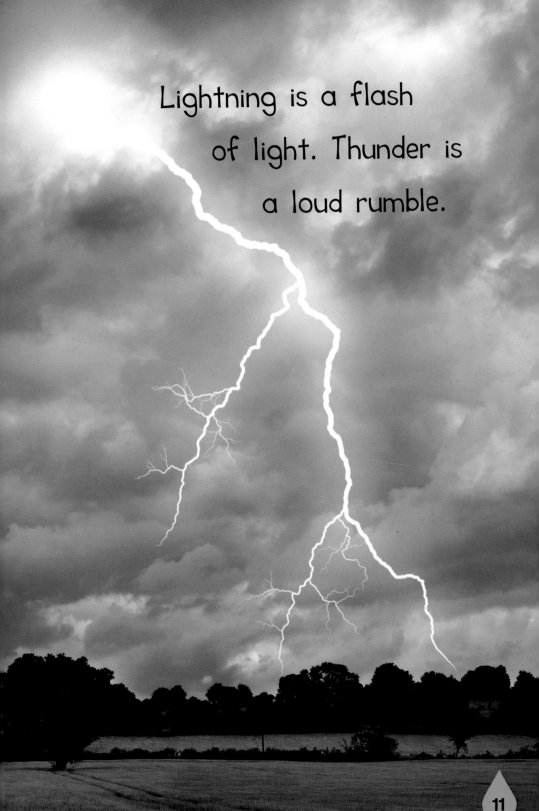

Lightning is a flash
of light. Thunder is
a loud rumble.

Too much rain

Heavy rain makes
rivers overflow.

The water rushes over the land. It can do a lot of harm. This is called a **flood**.

Not enough rain

If it does not rain for a while, plants cannot grow.

There may be
too little water
for everyone to
use. This is called
a **drought**.

Rain and plants

Trees, flowers and plants need rain to grow.

If it is hot and dry, you must water plants yourself.

Rainforests

Rainforests grow in hot places where it rains a lot.

Trees grow high into the sky. Plants grow all over the ground.

The plants grow quickly
because of all the rain.

Rainbows

Rainbows appear
in the sky when
the sun shines
through raindrops.

You only see
rainbows when
it is raining and
the sun is shining.

Fun in the rain

Splash! It's fun to play in puddles.

You can stay dry
by wearing a
waterproof coat
and wellies.
You can also
put up an
umbrella.

23

Glossary

cloud a group of water droplets in the air

drizzle light rain

drought a long time without rain

flood an overflow of water

lightning a flash of light in the sky

rainbow an arc of colours caused by sunlight shining through water droplets

rainforest a dense forest where a lot of rain falls

thunder the loud sound that comes after lightning

thunderstorm a storm with heavy rain, thunder and lightning

waterproof not allowing water to enter